Editor
Eric Migliaccio

Editor in Chief
Ina Massler Levin, M.A.

Cover Designer
Karen J. Goldfluss, M.S. Ed.

Cover Artist
Barb Lorseyedi

Creative Director
Karen J. Goldfluss, M.S. Ed.

Imaging
James Edward Grace
Craig Gunnell

CD Application Programmer
Charles Payne

Publisher
Mary D. Smith, M.S. Ed.

TCR 3419

for All INTERACTI

Paragraph Editing

CORRELATED TO COMMON CORE STANDARDS

studied
We ~~studyed~~ hummingbirds in
today   These
class ~~tooday. Theese~~ tiny birds
their
can flap ~~they~~ wings up to eighty
S
time˄ per second. This allow˄
they
them to hover in mid-air as ~~them~~
fee   a flower's nectar.

✳ Developed for ALL Interactive Whiteboards
✳ 100 ready-to-edit paragraphs to practice and review grammar, punctuation, and spelling
✳ Includes Common Core State Standards
Teacher Created Resources

Teacher Created Resources
6421 Industry Way
Westminster, CA 92683
www.teachercreated.com
ISBN: 978-1-4206-3419-8
© *2013 Teacher Created Resources*
Made in U.S.A.

Teacher Created Resources

Table of Contents

Introduction 2

Common Core State Standards. 3

About the CD. 4

About the Book 6

Grammar Rules 7

Unit Paragraphs. 12

Editing Marks. 112

Introduction

Imagine a classroom tool that could make grammar and spelling exciting and engaging for your students. *Paragraph Editing* is a program that has been designed to do all of this and more. Compatible with all interactive whiteboards, *Paragraph Editing* offers the many advantages of touchscreen technology and allows your students to participate in learning like never before.

Each *Paragraph Editing* CD comes loaded with the paragraphs from this book. The paragraphs are divided into 25 units, with new grammar rules incorporated into each of the first 15 units. In this way, grammar, punctuation, and spelling concepts are introduced and then reinforced in a systematic manner, allowing students to practice each concept before learning new ones. The final 10 units of each book and CD offer a cumulative reinforcement of all of the rules and concepts previously learned.

These paragraphs can be accessed and printed from the CD or copied from the book. They can be done as in-class work or assigned as homework. Corrections to these paragraphs can then be made on individual computers or on an interactive whiteboard in front of the class. All it takes is a finger or a special pen, depending on the interactive board you use. You and your students can correct the sentences in these ways:

☞ by writing and drawing directly onto the interactive whiteboard

☞ by grabbing punctuation stamps built into the program and dragging them over the corresponding errors

An array of buttons and menus allows you to do (and undo) every correction quickly and easily and in six custom colors. Best of all, it takes just one quick click of a button for teachers and students to see the correct answers. And, as an added teaching tool, another touch of a button will show students the locations of the paragraph's errors without revealing the actual answers.

In addition to the paragraphs included on the CD, the *Paragraph Editing* program allows you to create and save thousands of custom paragraphs. The program can even make incorrect versions of your custom creations by adding errors for you. Teachers can use this tool to tap into their class's creativity with student-generated paragraphs and peer-editing exercises.

Common Core State Standards

The activities in this book meet one or more of the following Common Core State Standards. © Copyright 2010. National Governors Association Center for Best Practices and Council of Chief State School Officers. All rights reserved. For more information about the Common Core State Standards, go to *http://www.corestandards.org/*.

Reading Standards: Foundational Skills
Fluency

Standard 1: RF.5.4. Demonstrate understanding of the organization and basic features of print.

- RF.5.4a: Read grade-level text with purpose and understanding.

- RF.5.4c: Use context to confirm or self-correct word recognition and understanding, rereading as necessary.

Language Standards
Conventions of Standard English

Standard 1: L.5.1 Demonstrate command of the conventions of standard English grammar and usage when writing or speaking.

- L.5.1b: Form and use the perfect (e.g., *I had walked*; *I have walked*; *I will have walked*) verb tenses.

- L.5.1d: Recognize and correct inappropriate shifts in verb tense.

Standard 2: L.5.2 Demonstrate command of the conventions of standard English capitalization, punctuation, and spelling when writing.

- L.5.2a: Use punctuation to separate items in a series.

- L.5.2b: Use a comma to separate an introductory element from the rest of the sentence.

- L.5.3c: Use a comma to set off the words *yes* and *no* (e.g., *Yes, thank you*), to set off a tag question from the rest of the sentence (e.g., *It's true, isn't it?*), and to indicate direct address (e.g., *Is that you, Steve?*).

- L.5.2d: Use underlining, quotation marks, or italics to indicate titles of works.

- L.5.2e: Spell grade-appropriate words correctly, consulting references as needed.

Vocabulary Acquisition and Use

Standard 4: L.5.4 Determine or clarify the meaning of unknown and multiple-meaning words and phrases based on grade 5 reading and content, choosing flexibly from a range of strategies.

- L.5.4a: Use context (e.g., cause/effect relationships and comparisons in text) as a clue to the meaning of a word or phrase.

About the CD

The real flexibility and interactivity of the *Paragraph Editing* program shine through in the resources included on the CD.

☞ Install the CD

Just pop the CD that accompanies this book into your PC or Mac, and you and your students can begin editing paragraphs at individual computers or on the interactive whiteboard in your classroom.

> **Quick Tip:** Step-by-step installation instructions and some troubleshooting tips are provided in the "ReadMe" file on the CD.

☞ The Main Menu

Once you have installed the CD, the Main Menu will appear on your computer screen or interactive whiteboard.

> **Quick Tip:** The Main Menu will open up in full-screen mode. If you wish to resize the Main Menu screen, hit the ESC button. This will allow you to adjust it as needed.

From the Main Menu, you can access all of the features and resources available in the program. To get a detailed explanation of these features, click on the Guide button. This will take you to the *Paragraph Editing* User's Guide.

☞ The User's Guide

Everything you need to know in order to use and operate the *Paragraph Editing* CD and program can be found in the User's Guide. This is also where you will find a useful one-page handout of the editing symbols used in the program. These marks are available as punctuation stamps on the editing screen for each sentence.

Main Menu Screen

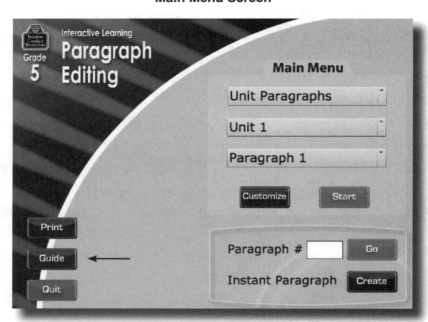

About the CD *(cont.)*

The User's Guide on the CD contains a lot of important and helpful information. However, you may wish to immediately begin editing paragraphs with your students. The following Quick-Start Guide will help you do just that.

Quick-Start Guide for Editing Paragraphs

1. **Launch the Program:** Load the CD and launch the program. If needed, follow the installation instructions given in the "ReadMe" file on the CD.

2. **Click the Start Button:** You can access the **Start** button from the **Main Menu** screen. (See the graphic to the right.) This will take you directly to the editing screen. (See the graphic at the bottom of the page.)

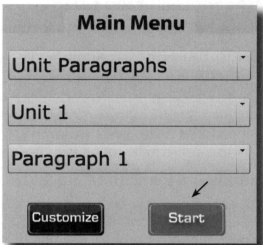

3. **Edit the Paragraph:** Write, draw, or paint directly onto the screen. You may also use the punctuation stamps located on either side of the screen. Grab, drag, and drop these stamps onto, above, or below the word to correct the errors.

4. **Check Your Work:** Click on the **Show Errors** button to give your students hints about where the errors can be found in the paragraph. Click on the **Show Correct** button to reveal the correct version of the paragraph.

5. **Edit a New Paragraph:** Click on the **Next** button to continue the editing lesson with a new paragraph.

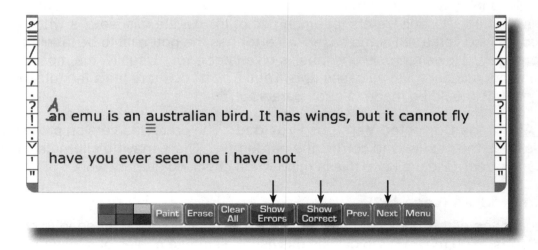

About the Book

There are two main components to the *Paragraph Editing* program: a book and a CD. These two parts were designed to be complementary, but they can also be used independently of one another. This 112-page book contains the following features:

☞ **Common Core State Standards (page 3)**

The grammar rules and concepts reviewed in this book meet Common Core State Standards for grade-level appropriateness.

☞ **Tips for Using the CD (pages 4–5)**

These two pages include tips for getting started with the CD that accompanies this book.

☞ **Grammar Rules (pages 7–11)**

This book includes a list of the punctuation, capitalization, and usage rules students will need to know in order to correct the paragraphs. New rules are introduced in each of the first 15 units, allowing students to learn increasingly difficult grammar concepts at a measured pace, while reviewing the ones they have previously learned. The final 10 units serve as a cumulative review of the rules learned in the first 15 units.

☞ **Ready-To-Be-Edited Paragraphs (pages 12–111)**

On each even-numbered page of this section, there are two error-filled paragraphs. (In all, this book contains a total of 100 unique paragraphs.) These paragraphs contain plenty of space between lines so students may add editing marks and rewrite incorrectly spelled words. Copy these pages for use as in-class assignments or send them home as homework.

On the odd-numbered pages that follow, the corrected versions of the paragraphs are given. The revisions are shown in gray, and a summary of the errors that can be found in each paragraph is provided.

<u>**Note About the Summary of Errors:**</u> The terms used in this list are meant to help you quickly locate specific types of errors. Many terms refer to both the omission and the misuse of that element. *Examples:* The term "Periods" is given when a period is missing and also when one is used incorrectly (in place of a question mark, for example). "Capitalization" is a broad term used to refer to any instance where a capital or lowercase letter is needed. "Usage" refers to, among other things, the misuse of *a* when *an* is needed, or vice versa. In some cases, an error has the potential to be labeled in more than one way. However, only one label is given per error. Usually, the most specific term has been chosen. In all cases, the "Total Errors" count reflects the total number of changes that should be made to each paragraph.

<u>**Note About the Corrected Versions Provided:**</u> The corrected version provided shows what is often the best way to correct the paragraph. There may be alternate ways that are also correct. Please keep this in mind when checking student work.

☞ **Editing Marks (page 112)**

The final page of this book contains a full list of the editing marks needed to correct the paragraphs. You may wish to display this list or distribute copies of it to your students.

Grammar Rules

The following pages include most of the grammar, usage, and punctuation rules students will need to know to edit the paragraphs in this book. The units in which these rules are applicable are listed in parentheses after each rule.

Rule 1: A *sentence* is a group of words that tells a complete thought. Capitalize the first word in a sentence. A *statement* is a sentence that tells something. Put a period at the end of a telling sentence. A *question* is a sentence that asks something. Put a question mark at the end of an asking sentence. An *exclamation* is a sentence that shows strong feeling. It ends with an exclamation mark. A *command* is a sentence that tells someone to do something. It ends with a period or an exclamation mark. **(Units 1–25)**

- **My dog is black.**
- **Do you have a pet?**
- **Please print your name.**
- **Get out of the street!**

Rule 2: Capitalize the word *I*. **(Units 1–25)**

- **Scott and I are friends.**

Rule 3: *Proper nouns* name specific people, places, and things. A proper noun begins with a capital letter. *Common nouns* are not specific. A common noun does not begin with a capital letter. **(Units 1–25)**

- **That dog is named Max.** (common noun = *dog*; proper noun = *Max*)

Rule 4: An *abbreviation* is a short form of a word. Capitalize name titles and put a period after ones that have been shortened into an abbreviation. Also capitalize and put a period after initials, which are letters used instead of a full name. Do not capitalize *a.m.* or *p.m.* **(Units 1–25)**

- **The building is owned by Mr. Payne and Dr. Anna Lee.**
- **The author of the book is J.P. Wilson.**
- **School starts at 7:00 a.m.**

Rule 5: Capitalize the days of the week, months of the year, and holidays. Do not capitalize seasons of the year. **(Units 1–25)**

- **My favorite season is spring.**
- **Is Memorial Day on a Monday in May?**

Rule 6: Use a comma to separate the day and year or to separate the day and month. Use a comma to separate a city and state or country. When these elements appear in the beginning or middle of a sentence, use a comma to separate them from the rest of the sentence. **(Units 1–25)**

- **She was born on Thursday, November 2, 2006.**
- **Andrea flew from Houston, Texas, to Paris, France.**
- **July 7, 2007, was the day we met.**

Rule 7: A *colon* is used between the hour and minutes when writing the time of day. **(Units 1–25)**

- **We went to school at 8:00.**

Grammar Rules (cont.)

Rule 8: A *run-on sentence* has two complete thoughts that run into each other. Use a period or other end punctuation to divide these thoughts into two sentences. (**Units 1–25**)

- **I woke up late my alarm clock is broken.** (*incorrect*)
- **I woke up late. My alarm clock is broken.** (*correct*)

Rule 9: A series is a list of three or more items. Use a comma to separate three or more words or groups of words in a series. (**Units 2–25**)

- **Would you rather have pizza, pasta, or a hamburger?**
- **We went to the beach, ate lunch, and saw a movie on Saturday.**

Rule 10: A *singular noun* names one person, place, thing, or idea. A *plural noun* names more than one person, place, thing, or idea. Add *s* to most nouns to make them plural. Add *es* to words that end in *s, ch, sh, x,* and *z.* (**Units 3–25**)

- **I have two small <u>dogs</u> and one big <u>dog</u>.**
- **I see one blue <u>dish</u> and two red <u>dishes</u>.**

Rule 11: Use *a* or *an* before singular nouns. Use *a* before words that begin with a consonant sound. Use *an* before words that begin with a vowel or vowel sound. (**Units 3–25**)

- **He ate <u>a</u> piece of toast and <u>an</u> egg <u>an</u> hour before school began.**

Rule 12: Nouns that end in the letter *y* have special rules for making plurals. If the word ends with a vowel followed by *y*, just add *s*. If the word ends with a consonant followed by *y*, change the *y* to *i* and add *es*. (**Units 4–25**)

- **Dad put his <u>keys</u> in his coat pocket.**
- **I went to two birthday <u>parties</u> in June.**

Rule 13: Nouns that end in *f* or *fe* also have a special rule for making plurals. In most words, change the *f* or *fe* to *v* and add *es*. Other plural nouns are formed in an irregular way (like *children* and *feet*), while other nouns don't change their form at all when pluralized (like *fish* and *sheep*). (**Units 4–25**)

- **One <u>calf</u> has black spots. Two <u>calves</u> have brown spots.**
- **One <u>child</u> has one <u>fish</u>. Two <u>children</u> have two <u>fish</u>.**

Rule 14: A *possessive noun* shows ownership. Use an *apostrophe* and an *s* (*'s*) after a noun to show that something belongs to one person, group, or thing. To form the plural possessive of a plural noun that ends in *s*, add only an apostrophe. If the plural noun does not end in *s*, add an apostrophe and an *s*. (**Units 5–25**)

- **<u>Beth's</u> guitar is sitting next to <u>Jess's</u> drum set.**
- **Both of his <u>brothers'</u> bikes are blue.**
- **We visited the <u>children's</u> library yesterday.**

Grammar Rules *(cont.)*

Rule 15: A pronoun is a word that is used in place of a noun. Use the pronouns *I* and *me* correctly. Use the pronoun *I* when you are doing something. Use the pronoun *me* when something happens to you. **(Units 6–25)**

- **Mom and I went to Hawaii.   She waved to Bob and me.**

Rule 16: Use the personal pronouns *we/us, she/he, her/him,* and *they/them* correctly. Also use possessive pronouns (e.g., *mine, ours, his, hers, its, theirs*) and reflexive pronouns (e.g., *myself, herself, themselves*) correctly. **(Units 6–25)**

- **We went to the park. Sam took us there.**
- **They ate the pie that she baked for them.**
- **They gave the trophy to us. The trophy is ours.**
- **Sue bought herself the bike. The bike is hers now.**

Rule 17: A *contraction* is a word made by joining two words. When joining the words, a letter or letters are left out. An apostrophe is put in the word at the spot where the letter or letters are missing. **(Units 7–25)**

- **We are going home.   We're going home.**
- **She did not see him.   She didn't see him.**
- **He will be there soon.   He'll be there soon.**

Rule 18: A name can be made into a contraction or a possessive by adding *'s.* The *'s* can mean "is" or "has," depending on the sentence. **(Units 7–25)**

- **Mary's going to Canada this summer.** *(contraction for "Mary is")*
- **Mary's been packing for her trip.** *(contraction for "Mary has")*
- **I saw Mary's car parked in the lot.** *(possessive)*

Rule 19: The verb often shows the action of the sentence. When the subject of the sentence is singular, an *s* or *es* is usually added to the verb (except with the pronouns *I* or *you*.) When the subject is plural, an *s* is not added to the verb. **(Units 8–25)**

- **Ryan eats a lot of food. Eric and Bob eat more food. I eat the most food.**
- **The school fixes lunch for us. They fix lunch for us every day.**

Rule 20: The verbs *am, are, is, was,* and *were* are forms of the word *be.* They are not action words. Instead, they tell what someone or something is like. Use "am" with the word "I." Use "is" and "are" when talking about what is happening now. Use "was" and "were" when talking about things that have already happened. Use "is" and "was" when talking about one person, place, thing, or idea. Use "are" and "were" when talking about more than one person, place, thing, or idea, and with the word "you." **(Units 8–25)**

- **I am six years old. You are older than I am.**
- **Jim is seven years old. Last year, Jim was six.**
- **Kate and Nate are eight. They were seven last year.**

Grammar Rules *(cont.)*

Rule 21: A *present-tense verb* shows action that happens now. A *past-tense verb* tells about an action that already happened. Add *ed* to most verbs to form the past tense. In addition to *s* and *es*, the ending *ing* can also be added to present-tense verbs. If the verb has a single vowel and ends with a consonant, the last consonant is usually doubled before adding *ed* or *ing*. If the word ends with a silent *e*, drop the final *e* before adding *ed* or *ing*. **(Units 8–25)**

- **The car <u>stops</u> here now. It also <u>stopped</u> here yesterday. Will it be <u>stopping</u> here every day?**
- **I <u>wave</u> goodbye. I <u>waved</u> to everybody. I am <u>waving</u> my hand.**

Rule 22: If a verb ends with a consonant and *y*, change the *y* to *i* and add *es* to form the present-tense verb. If a verb ends with a consonant and *y*, change the *y* to *i* and add *ed* to form a past-tense verb. **(Units 8–25)**

- **Each team <u>tries</u> to win.   I <u>tried</u> to hit a home run.**

Rule 23: The past tense of some verbs is made by changing the spelling. **(Units 8–25)**

- **Last week my dog <u>ran</u> away.** *(run)*
- **He <u>bought</u> some milk at the store.** *(buy)*
- **He <u>drew</u> a picture in art class.** *(draw)*

Rule 24: Helping verbs are sometimes used with main action verbs. Some examples of helping verbs are *has, have, had, is, are, was, were,* and *will.* **(Units 8–25)**

- **Yesterday I saw you at the mall. I <u>have seen</u> you there before.**
- **We <u>were</u> eating dinner when you called.**

Rule 25: An *adjective* is a word that describes a noun or a pronoun. Add *er* to most adjectives to compare two people, places, things, etc. Add *est* to compare more than two. **(Units 9–25)**

- **Lee is <u>taller</u> than Joe. In fact, Lee is the <u>tallest</u> student in the class.**

Rule 26: Commas are used to separate some elements in a sentence. **(Units 10–25)**

Use a comma after "yes" or "no" at the beginning of a sentence.

- **<u>Yes,</u> I am going to the store. <u>No,</u> you are not.**

Use a comma to separate introductory words or phrases at the beginning of a sentence.

- **<u>Wow,</u> it's hot today! <u>Well,</u> it was hotter yesterday.**
- **<u>If I remember correctly,</u> it was cold and rainy last week.**

Use a comma to set off the name of a person being directly addressed or described.

- **<u>Bill,</u> are you going to the party? Yes,<u> Tim,</u> I am.**

Use a comma to set off words like *however* and *though* and the word *too* when meaning "also."

- **I, <u>too,</u> want to go to the movies. <u>However,</u> I have too much homework.**

our family drove through arizona on our way to

dallas, Texas. We decided to visit the Grand canyon

along the way. What an amazing place. We would

all like to go there ~~agin~~ *again* some day?

Unit 1 • Paragraph 1 Errors

Capitalization 4
Commas 1
Exclamation
 Points 1
Periods 2
Spelling 1

Total Errors: 9

Robert J. clark teaches Math at Park Ave. high

School in springville, utah. He was hired on august

17, 1963. Mr. Clark is planning to retire at the end

of the ~~skool~~ *school* year.

Unit 1 • Paragraph 2 Errors

Capitalization 6
Commas 2
Periods 4
Spelling 1

Total Errors: 13

Kayla and her friend C J met at parkfield theater last thursday night. They saw a moovie at 830 pm. Then they went to get some ice cream at a place called tasty Treats

our soccer team willl be playing in the championship game at fairfax field on Saturday october 9. The game starts at 130 I hope aunt Annie and Uncle fred can be there. They alwways bring me good luck

Kayla and her friend **C. J.** met at **parkfield theater** last **thursday** night. They saw a ~~moovie~~ *movie* at **830 pm.** Then they went to get some ice cream at a place called **tasty Treats.**

Unit 1 • Paragraph 3 Errors

Capitalization	4
Colons	1
Periods	4
Spelling	1

Total Errors: 10

our soccer team **will** be playing in the championship game at **fairfax field** on **Saturday, october** 9. The game starts at **130.** I hope **aunt** **Annie** and **Uncle fred** can be there. They ~~alwways~~ *always* bring me good **luck.**

Unit 1 • Paragraph 4 Errors

Capitalization	6
Colons	1
Commas	1
Periods	2
Spelling	2

Total Errors: 12

my little sister always draws with the same

three colorrs. She uses blue purple and pink every

time. I have tried to convince her that other colors

are nice i am tired of looking at blu dogs purpel

cats and pink fish!

My friends and i are starting a band Craig

will play the drums Allie will play the bass, and

paul will play the guitar. I will singg and play

the piano. craig allie Paul and I will make great

music The four of us have been freinds for years.

my little sister always draws with the same

three colorrs. [colors] She uses blue, purple, and pink every

time. I have tried to convince her that other colors

are nice. i am tired of looking at blu [blue] dogs, purpel [purple]

cats, and pink fish!

**Unit 2 • Paragraph 5
Errors**

Capitalization 2
Commas. 4
Periods. 1
Spelling 3

Total Errors: 10

My friends and i are starting a band. Craig

will play the drums. Allie will play the bass, and

paul will play the guitar. I will sings [sing] and play

the piano. craig, allie, Paul, and I will make great

music. The four of us have been freinds [friends] for years.

**Unit 2 • Paragraph 6
Errors**

Capitalization 4
Commas. 4
Periods. 2
Spelling 2

Total Errors: 12

The Kent family traveled to europe last Summer. They visited England france and spain Clara kent said that her favoritt place was Paris France. She luvved looking down at the city from the top of the eiffel Tower

have you ever gotten goose bumps. These bumps show up on your skin when you are feeling cold scared or other intense emotions. tiny musscles pull your hairs up The skin around the hair bunches up. This traps air neer your body and helps keep u warm

The Kent family traveled to europe last

Summer. They visited England, france, and spain.

Clara kent said that her favorite place was Paris,

France. She ~~luvved~~ loved looking down at the city from

the top of the eiffel Tower.

Unit 2 • Paragraph 7
Errors

Capitalization 6
Commas........ 3
Periods......... 2
Spelling 2

Total Errors: 13

have you ever gotten goose bumps. These

bumps show up on your skin when you are feeling

cold, scared, or other intense emotions. tiny

~~musscles~~ muscles pull your hairs up. The skin around the

hair bunches up. This traps air ~~neer~~ near your body

and helps keep ~~u~~ you warm.

Unit 2 • Paragraph 8
Errors

Capitalization 2
Commas........ 2
Periods......... 2
Question
  Marks........ 1
Spelling 3

Total Errors: 10

~~~~~~

What a amazing day. We went on a class field trip to the san diego Zoo. We saw many lions gorilla, and snake. I watched a elephant use its trunks to spray water i also got to watch two foxs playing with eech other.

~~~~~~

I helped the smiths move into their new home at 223 spring St in Ames Iowa. I earned fifty dollar for three hour of work. I helped lift two table a old couch and an huge refrigerator I must have carried forty boxs of books, too.

What a[n] amazing day[!] We went on a class field trip to the san diego Zoo. We saw many lions[,] gorilla[s], and snake[s]. I watched a[n] elephant use its trunks to spray water[.] [I] also got to watch two foxs playing with ~~each~~ [each] other.

Unit 3 • Paragraph 9 Errors

Capitalization	3
Commas	1
Exclamation Points	1
Periods	1
Plurals	4
Spelling	1
Usage	2

Total Errors: 13

I helped the smiths move into their new home at 223 spring St[.] in Ames[,] Iowa. I earned fifty dollar[s] for three hour[s] of work. I helped lift two table[s] a[n] old couch[,] and a[n] huge refrigerator[.] I must have carried forty boxs of books, too.

Unit 3 • Paragraph 10 Errors

Capitalization	2
Comma	3
Periods	2
Plurals	4
Usage	2

Total Errors: 13

What do u think is the tastiest fruit. Is it a apple a banana or a orange. My friend patty says that peachs are her favorite She bought six basket of them at that orchard on Elm ave last summer.

I must take two bus to get to school. The first buss arrives at 720. It picks me up at the corner of olive ave. and carson St I meet two of my friend at the Downey Rd bus stop at 7.35. An secund bus picks us up there.

What do u think is the tastiest fruit. Is it a [you] [?] [n]

apple a banana or a orange. My friend patty says [n] [?]

that peachs are her favorite. She bought six basket [e] [s]

of them at that orchard on Elm ave. last summer.

**Unit 3 • Paragraph 11
Errors**

Capitalization 2
Commas 2
Periods 2
Plurals 2
Question
  Marks 2
Spelling 1
Usage 2

Total Errors: 13

I must take two bus to get to school. The [es]

first buss arrives at 720. It picks me up at the

corner of olive ave. and carson St. I meet two of

my friend at the Downey Rd. bus stop at 7.35. [s]

An second bus picks us up there. [second]

**Unit 3 • Paragraph 12
Errors**

Capitalization 3
Colons 2
Periods 2
Plurals 2
Spelling 2
Usage 1

Total Errors: 12

it is my job to set the table each night I begin by putting out dishs for Mom, dad, jane, and meself. then I fold the napkins and place those nexxt to the plates. I finish by putting forks spoons knifes and glasss at each setting

Grover jones is the tallest person in our town. He is almost seven foots tall That is gigantic? People always ask Grover how the weather is up near the ceeling. grover just smiles. he is allso one of the nicest person in our townn.

it is my job to set the table each night. I

begin by putting out dishs *(e)* for Mom, dad, jane,

and meself. *myself* then I fold the napkins and place

those nexxt *next* to the plates. I finish by putting

forks, spoons, knifes *knives* and glasss *(e)* at each setting.

Unit 4 • Paragraph 13
Errors

Capitalization 4
Commas. 3
Periods. 2
Plurals 3
Spelling 2

Total Errors: 14

Grover jones is the tallest person in our town.

He is almost seven foots *feet* tall. That is gigantic!

People always ask Grover how the weather is up

near the ceeling. *ceiling* grover just smiles. he is allso *also*

one of the nicest person *people* in our townn. *town*

Unit 4 • Paragraph 14
Errors

Capitalization 3
Exclamation
  Points. 1
Periods. 1
Plurals 2
Spelling 3

Total Errors: 10

Name: _____ Date: _____

I checked my pokkets to see how much change I have i found a quarter three dime, and five pennys. I added up theese numbers. They equall 60 cent. Then my friend todd gave me six nickles. How much money do I have now.

My little brother and i pretended we were monkey. We swung frum the bars in the playground. he scratched under his armpits and made monkey sound. I ate a imaginary banana. Then our mom told us it was time to eat our lunchs we had turkey sandwichs crackers and apple juice.

I checked my ~~pokkets~~ pockets to see how much change I have. i found a quarter, three dime**s**, and five ~~pennys~~ pennies. I added up ~~theese~~ these numbers. They equall. 60 cent**s**. Then my friend todd gave me six ~~nickies~~ nickels. How much money do I have now?

Unit 4 • Paragraph 15 Errors

Capitalization 2
Commas 1
Periods 1
Plurals 3
Question
  Marks 1
Spelling 4

Total Errors: 12

My little brother and i pretended we were monkey**s**. We swung ~~frum~~ from the bars in the playground. he scratched under his armpits and made monkey sound**s**. I ate a**n** imaginary banana. Then our mom told us it was time to eat our lunch**es**. we had turkey sandwich**es**, crackers, and apple juice.

Unit 4 • Paragraph 16 Errors

Capitalization 3
Commas 2
Periods 1
Plurals 4
Spelling 1
Usage 1

Total Errors: 12

our nieghbor Todd Williams goes to kennedy

high school. He is the quarterback on the schools

football team. We watched one of Todds game last

friday night. He threw three touchdown pass and

ledd his team to victory?

I pet two playful puppys at pine park

yesterday. Both of the puppies tails wagged when

I pett them. They seemed lost. I checked both

dog's collars and found tag. The tags said that

the puppyies belonged to Mr and Mrs Sampson

of Ft worth texas.

~~~~~~~~~~~~~~~~~~~~~~~~~~~~~~~~~~

neighbor

our ~~nieghbor~~ Todd Williams goes to kennedy

high school. He is the quarterback on the schools'

football team. We watched one of Todd's game*s* last

friday night. He threw three touchdown pass*es* and

led. his team to victory?.

Unit 5 • Paragraph 17
Errors

Apostrophes 2
Capitalization 5
Periods 1
Plurals 2
Spelling 2

Total Errors: 12

~~~~~~~~~~~~~~~~~~~~~~~~~~~~~~~~~~

puppies

I pet two playful ~~puppys~~ at pine park

yesterday. Both of the puppies' tails wagged when

I pet. them. They seemed lost. I checked both

dogs'

~~dog's~~ collars and found tag*s*. The tags said that

puppies

the ~~puppyies~~ belonged to Mr. and Mrs. Sampson

of Ft. worth, texas.

Unit 5 • Paragraph 18
Errors

Apostrophes 2
Capitalization 4
Commas 1
Periods 3
Plurals 3
Spelling 1

Total Errors: 14

Tims mom took us to the Ocean valley Aquarium on thursday. I have never seen so many fishes before in my Life? I had nevver been to a aquarium beforr. I saw many seals walrus, and otters I even got a good look at a sharks sharp tooths!

ostriches are unusual birds. They cannot fly, but they can run verry fast. Would you have guessed that ostrichs are the worlds fastest two-legged animals That is surpprising for such a large Bird. A ostriches weight can reech over 300 pound.

Tim's mom took us to the Ocean valley

Aquarium on thursday. I have never seen so many

fishes before in my Life? I had *never* been to a[n]

aquarium before. I saw many seals, walrus[es] and

otters. I even got a good look at a shark's sharp

teeth
~~tooths~~!

Unit 5 • Paragraph 19
Errors

Apostrophes	2
Capitalization	3
Commas	1
Exclamation Points	1
Periods	1
Plurals	3
Spelling	2
Usage	1

Total Errors: 14

ostriches are unusual birds. They cannot fly,

but they can run *very* fast. Would you have

guessed that ostrich[es] are the world's fastest

two-legged animals? That is ~~surprising~~ *surprising* for such

a large Bird. A[n] ostrich's weight can ~~reech~~ *reach* over

300 pound[s].

Unit 5 • Paragraph 20
Errors

Apostrophes	2
Capitalization	2
Plurals	2
Question Marks	1
Spelling	3
Usage	1

Total Errors: 11

My family and me live near sunrise beach. My friends love to visit me and go swimming in the ocean. Jan ella and mike are me three best friend. Them come over offen. My sisters freinds are here even more. Her and they go to the beach allmost every day?

My neighbors name is Mrs pierce. Her has many pets I have seen six cats three dogs, and one furry rabbits running around she's house. A aquarium in her kichen is home to about twenty fishs. She lets me brother and I come over and play with the animal.

My family and ~~me~~ live near sunrise beach. My [I]

friends love to visit me and go swimming in the

ocean. Jan ella and mike are me three best [y]

friend. Them come over ~~offen~~. My sisters ~~freinds~~ [s] [y] [often] [friends]

are here even more. ~~Her~~ and they go to the [She]

beach ~~allmost~~ every day? [almost] [!]

Unit 6 • Paragraph 21
Errors

Apostrophes 1
Capitalization 4
Commas........ 2
Exclamation
  Points......... 1
Plurals 1
Pronouns 4
Spelling 3

Total Errors: 16

My neighbors name is Mrs pierce. ~~Her~~ has [She]

many pets I have seen six cats three dogs, and

one furry rabbits running around ~~she's~~ house. A [her] [n]

aquarium in her kichen is home to about twenty [t]

fishs. She lets ~~me~~ brother and I come over and [s] [my] [me]

play with the animal. [s]

Unit 6 • Paragraph 22
Errors

Apostrophes 1
Capitalization 1
Commas........ 1
Periods......... 2
Plurals 3
Pronouns 4
Spelling 1
Usage 1

Total Errors: 14

~~~~~~

   Mom and Dad said that I could have a nu

computer if i gave me old one to my little sister

and showed her how to use them. My sisters name

is chloe. Chloes face lit up when her heard the

plann. My old computter is her's now

~~~~~~

   Rod And Todd wilson are twin brother who just

started atttending our school. Mr hill asked we to

treet our new classmates well. Both brothers desks

are right near my. I introduced meself and told

them i was here to help. Them both smiled and

thanked me?

Mom and Dad said that I could have a ~~nu~~ ^new^

computer if i gave me old one to my little sister

and showed her how to use ~~them.~~ ^it^ My sisters name

is chloe. Chloes face lit up when ~~her~~ ^she^ heard the

plano. My old ~~computter~~ ^computer^ is ~~her's~~ ^hers^ now⊙

**Unit 6 • Paragraph 23
Errors**

Apostrophes 2
Capitalization 2
Periods 1
Pronouns 4
Spelling 3

Total Errors: 12

Rod And Todd wilson are twin brother^s^ who just

started attending our school. Mr⊙ hill asked ~~we~~ ^us^ to

treat our new classmates well. Both brothers' desks

are right near ~~my.~~ ^mine^ I introduced m^y^self and told

them i was here to help. Them^y^ both smiled and

thanked me⊙

**Unit 6 • Paragraph 24
Errors**

Apostrophes 1
Capitalization 4
Periods 2
Plurals 1
Pronouns 4
Spelling 2

Total Errors: 14

Drew Kate and me each wore a diferent color shirt Today. Drews shirt was red Kates was white, and my was green All three of we wore blu jeans. Weve all decided to wear our black shirt tommorrow.

Qwans friend is named Bobby. Bobbys coming on a trip to summerville this Spring with, Qwan, Kelly, and I. Were all very exxcited. Ive never met Bobby, but I hope him is up for a adventure. Well be doing a lot of fun thing on the trip

Drew, Kate, and me each wore a diferent color shirt Today. Drews shirt was red, Kates was white, and my was green All three of we wore blu jeans. We've all decided to wear our black shirt tommorrow.

Unit 7 • Paragraph 25 Errors

Apostrophes	3
Capitalization	1
Commas	3
Periods	1
Plurals	1
Pronouns	3
Spelling	3

Total Errors: 15

Qwans friend is named Bobby. Bobbys coming on a trip to summerville this Spring with, Qwan, Kelly, and I. Were all very exxcited. Ive never met Bobby, but I hope him is up for a adventure. Well be doing a lot of fun thing on the trip.

Unit 7 • Paragraph 26 Errors

Apostrophes	5
Capitalization	2
Commas	1
Periods	1
Plurals	1
Pronouns	2
Spelling	1
Usage	1

Total Errors: 14

Do you know whos running for class pressident this year. Im hoping that Shelly garcia decides to run. Id vote for her ten time if I could. Shes very friendly extreemly smart and full of great idea. Who would you votte for

Our new neighbors niece is named nora nealy. Shes about the same age as i am. Nora vissits her Aunts house after school every day. I told her that theres a soccer game every Tuesday and Fryday. Us play for at leest a hour or until it gets dark

Do you know whos running for class pressident

this year. Im hoping that Shelly garcia decides to

run. Id vote for her ten time if I could. Shes very

friendly extreemly smart and full of great idea.

Who would you votte for

Unit 7 • Paragraph 27 Errors	
Apostrophes	4
Capitalization	1
Commas	2
Plurals	2
Question Marks	2
Spelling	3

Total Errors: 14

Our new neighbors niece is named nora nealy.

Shes about the same age as i am. Nora vissits

her Aunts house after school every day. I told her

that theres a soccer game every Tuesday and

Fryday. Us play for at leest a hour or until it

gets dark

Unit 7 • Paragraph 28 Errors	
Apostrophes	4
Capitalization	4
Periods	1
Pronouns	1
Spelling	3
Usage	1

Total Errors: 14

Unit 8
Paragraph
29

Willy will be attending two partys in february His friend phil is celebrateing his birthday on sunday Febuary 12. His cousin lacy is getting marryed on the 19th. That are two Sunday in a row that willy will need to wher nice clothes.

Unit 8
Paragraph
30

P.J and me spended last Summer at Bear Claw Camp. Her and I learnd to hike fish and build fires. Hikeing was my favorite activvity. PJ was very skilld at building fires. She once builded a fire by useing only her hands and two stick. I were impressed.

Willy will be attending two ~~partys~~ *parties* in ~~february~~. *(period)*

His friend ~~phil~~ is celebrat~~e~~ing his birthday on

~~sunday~~ ^r^ Febuary 12. His cousin ~~lacy~~ is getting

marr~~y~~ied on the 19th. That ~~are~~ *is* two Sunday *s* in a

row that ~~willy~~ will need to ~~wher~~ *wear* nice clothes.

Unit 8 • Paragraph 29
Errors

Capitalization 5
Commas. 1
Periods. 1
Plurals 2
Spelling 2
Verbs 3

Total Errors: 14

P.J. and ~~me spended~~ *I spent* last **S**ummer at Bear Claw

Camp. ~~Her~~ *She* and I learn~~d~~ *e* to hike, fish, and build fires.

Hik~~e~~ing was my favorite activ~~v~~ity. **PJ.** was very

skill~~d~~ *e* at building fires. She once ~~builded~~ *built* a

fire by us~~e~~ing only her hands and two stick *s*.

I ~~were~~ *was* impressed.

Unit 8 • Paragraph 30
Errors

Capitalization 1
Commas. 2
Periods. 3
Plurals 1
Pronouns 2
Spelling 1
Verbs 7

Total Errors: 17

~~~~~~

We studyed hummingbirds in class tooday.

Theese tiny birds can flap they wings up to eighty

time per second This skill allow them to hover

in mid-air as them feed on a flowers nectar.

What a incredible sight to seen?

~~~~~~

uncle Pete has been liveing near Dallas Texas

for over fourty years. My brothers and me has

visited him many time. Weve goed to watch the

dallas Cowboys play a game twice. The stadium

where the cowboys play is really cool. It's got

the biggest TV screen Ive ever saw. Its huge

We studyed hummingbirds in class tooday.

Theese tiny birds can flap their ~~they~~ wings up to eighty

times per second. This skill allows them to hover

in mid-air as they feed on a flowers nectar.

What an incredible sight to seen?!

Unit 8 • Paragraph 31 Errors

Apostrophes 1
Exclamation
  Points........ 1
Periods......... 1
Plurals 1
Pronouns 2
Spelling 2
Usage 1
Verbs 3

Total Errors: 12

---

uncle Pete has been liveing near Dallas, Texas,

for over foŭrty years. My brothers and ~~me has~~ I have

visited him many times. We've ~~goed~~ gone to watch the

dallas Cowboys play a game twice. The stadium

where the cowboys play is really cool. It's got

the biggest TV screen I've ever ~~saw.~~ seen. Its huge!

Unit 8 • Paragraph 32 Errors

Apostrophes 3
Capitalization 3
Commas........ 2
Exclamation
  Points......... 1
Plurals 1
Pronouns 1
Spelling 1
Verbs 4

Total Errors: 16

There is three children in the Pratt family. Rosie is the younger. She is five year old. Mark is the oldest of the childs. He turnd twelve last week. Nick pratt is in the middel. Him and I am in mrs Warners class together. We is the goodest of friends.

My report today was on abraham lincoln. I beginned by stateing that I think Lincoln is the greater of all U.S presidents. His brave leadership helpt the nation thru a incredibly tuff time. His beliefs and actions leaded to the freeeing of the slaves. Him's death on April 15 1865 was a tragic day in american history.

There ~~is~~ (are) three children in the Pratt family.

Rosie is the ~~younger~~ (youngest). She is five year(s) old. Mark is the oldest of the ~~childs~~ (children). He turn(e)d twelve last week. Nick pratt is in the ~~middel~~ (middle). ~~Him~~ (He) and I ~~am~~ (are) in mrs. Warner's class together. We ~~is~~ (are) the ~~goodest~~ (best) of friends.

Unit 9 • Paragraph 33
Errors

Adjectives	2
Apostrophes	1
Capitalization	2
Periods	1
Plurals	2
Pronouns	1
Spelling	1
Verbs	4

Total Errors: 14

My report today was on abraham lincoln. I ~~beginned~~ (began) by stat(e)ing that I think Lincoln is the ~~greater~~ (greatest) of all U.S. presidents. His brave leadership ~~helpt~~ (helped) the nation ~~thru~~ (through) a(n) incredibly ~~tuff~~ (tough) time. His beliefs and actions ~~leaded~~ (led) to the free(e)ing of the slaves. ~~Him's~~ (His) death on April 15, 1865, was a tragic day in american history.

Unit 9 • Paragraph 34
Errors

Adjectives	1
Capitalization	3
Commas	2
Periods	1
Pronouns	1
Spelling	3
Usage	1
Verbs	4

Total Errors: 16

Did u know that giraffes has the higher blood pressure of any animal. Its because them have the longliest necks. A giraffes heart have to work hardest than other animals hearts to pump bludd. Can you name any other unyoosual facts about giraffe.

My buddys and me each buyed tennis racquet yesterday. Steven's racquet was the heavyest Kens racquet was the priciest and mine was the easier to swing. Mine racquet was pricyer than Stevens but much cheapper than ken's. Im sure that I maked the bestest purchase

you
Did ~~a~~ know that giraffes ~~has~~ the ~~higher~~ blood
have   highest

pressure of any animal. Its because them have the
?   y

longest
~~longliest~~ necks. A giraffes heart ~~have~~ to work
has

harder
~~hardest~~ than other animals hearts to pump ~~bludd~~.
blood

unusual
Can you name any other ~~unyoosual~~ facts about

s?
giraffe.

Unit 9 • Paragraph 35
Errors

Adjectives 3
Apostrophes 3
Plurals 1
Pronouns 1
Question
  Marks 2
Spelling 3
Verbs 2

Total Errors: 15

buddies   I   bought   s
My ~~buddys~~ and ~~me~~ each ~~buyed~~ tennis racquet

i
yesterday. Steven's racquet was the heavyest Kens

easiest
racquet was the priciest and mine was the ~~easier~~

My   i
to swing. ~~Mine~~ racquet was pricyer than Stevens

but much cheapper than ken's. Im sure that I

made   best
~~maked~~ the ~~bestest~~ purchase

Unit 9 • Paragraph 36
Errors

Adjectives 5
Apostrophes 3
Capitalization 1
Commas 2
Periods 1
Plurals 2
Pronouns 2
Verbs 2

Total Errors: 18

Can you imagine what roades would be like without traffic signals. Wow that would be so unsafe? Its a good thing that a policemen named lester wire invented the first electric traffic light in 1912. Him's invenshun only has red and green lights though. A improved version that includded yellow were created in 1920.

spiders frightin so many person. Them cant even stanned the sight of the tinier of spider crawling along the wall. I too used to be very frightend. Then I buyed a pet tarantula and named him harry. Harry you have change mine opinion of spiders forever.

Can you imagine what roades would be like without traffic signals. Wow that would be so unsafe? Its a good thing that a policemen named lester wire invented the first electric traffic light in 1912. Him's invenshun only has red and green lights though. A improved version that included yellow were created in 1920.

Unit 10 • Paragraph 37
Errors

Apostrophes	1
Capitalization	2
Commas	2
Exclamation Points	1
Plurals	2
Pronouns	1
Question Marks	1
Spelling	1
Usage	1
Verbs	3

Total Errors: 15

spiders frightin so many person. Them cant even stanned the sight of the tinier of spider crawling along the wall. I too used to be very frightend. Then I buyed a pet tarantula and named him harry. Harry you have change mine opinion of spiders forever.

Unit 10 • Paragraph 38
Errors

Adjectives	1
Apostrophes	1
Capitalization	2
Commas	3
Plurals	2
Pronouns	2
Spelling	3
Verbs	2

Total Errors: 16

Was Benjamin franklin ever the president of the

United states. No he was not. He done so many

other importent thing though. Franklin were a

author a politician, a sientist, and a inventor. He

was allso his countrys first postmaster general

Unfortunately this always happens. I open my

sootcase to pack for a trips. At some point my

two cats deside to jump in. I dont notice. Then

i get on a plane on a train or in a car Finally

I getting to where I'm going. Thats when I

disscover two little surprise waitting for me.

Was Benjamin franklin ever the president of the

United states, No he was not. He done so many
did

other important thing though. Franklin were a
a *s* *was* *n*

author a politician, a sientist, and a inventor. He
c *n*

was aliso his countrys first postmaster general
s

Unit 10 • Paragraph 39 Errors

Apostrophes 1
Capitalization 2
Commas. 3
Periods. 1
Plurals 1
Question
  Marks. 1
Spelling 3
Usage 2
Verbs 2

Total Errors: 16

Unfortunately this always happens. I open my

sootcase to pack for a trips. At some point my
suitcase

two cats deside to jump in. I dont notice. Then
c

i get on a plane on a train or in a car. Finally
i

I getting to where I'm going. Thats when I
get

disscover two little surprise waiting for me.
s

Unit 10 • Paragraph 40 Errors

Apostrophes 2
Capitalization 1
Commas. 5
Periods. 1
Plurals 2
Spelling 3
Verbs 2

Total Errors: 16

~~~~~~

Who can name the fastest land animal." asked

Mr Martin. Caleb raise his hand. Is it the cheetah,

he aksed. "That is correct, sayed Mr. martin. He

continued "The Cheetah can reach speeds of up to

70 mile per hour. No other land aminal is fastest.

~~~~~~

Tim asked Mike and me, Will you two be at

hockey tryouts on monday. "Yes Tim" I answerred.

Then mike said, I hope Coach smith times our

skateing. Ive been working on my speed a lot.

I wouldnt be surprised if i'm the faster skater

on the team this years.

"Who can name the fastest land animal," asked

Mr. Martin. Caleb raise[d] his hand. "Is it the cheetah,"

he aksed. "That is correct, sayed Mr. martin. He

continued, "The Cheetah can reach speeds of up to

70 mile[s] per hour. No other land aminal is fastest."

(margin corrections: asked, said, animal, faster)

Unit 11 • Paragraph 41
Errors

Adjectives	1
Capitalization	2
Commas	1
Periods	1
Plurals	1
Question Marks	2
Quotation Marks	5
Spelling	2
Verbs	2

Total Errors: 17

Tim asked Mike and me, "Will you two be at

hockey tryouts on monday? "Yes, Tim," I answered.

Then mike said, "I hope Coach smith times our

skateing. I've been working on my speed a lot.

I wouldn't be surprised if i'm the faster skater

on the team this years."

(margin corrections: fastest)

Unit 11 • Paragraph 42
Errors

Adjectives	1
Apostrophes	2
Capitalization	4
Commas	2
Plurals	1
Question Marks	1
Quotation Marks	4
Verbs	2

Total Errors: 17

I has never climbed this hi before, said Rosa. She was restting on a ridge on the north side of Mt watson. Her and Ted was halfway up the mountinn. Ted shaked his head and said Wait untill we getting to the top. The view up there is thrilling!

Ed sayed "Im thinking about a state in the United states. This U.S state is the larger of all 50 state. However this states population is very small. Only three other states has fewer person living in them Can you name this state." Is it alaska? askd Al?

Paragraph 43 (with editing marks)

"I ~~has~~ *have* never climbed this ~~hi~~ *high* before," said Rosa. She was res~~t~~ting on a ridge on the north side of Mt. watson. ~~Her~~ *She* and Ted ~~was~~ *were* halfway up the ~~mountinn~~ *mountain*. Ted ~~shaked~~ *shook* his head and said "Wait until we ~~getting~~ *get* to the top. The view up there is thrilling!"

Unit 11 • Paragraph 43
Errors

Capitalization 1
Commas........ 1
Periods......... 1
Pronouns 1
Quotation
  Marks 4
Spelling 3
Verbs 5

Total Errors: 16

Paragraph 44 (with editing marks)

Ed ~~sayed~~ *said* "Im thinking about a state in the United states. This U.S. state is the ~~larger~~ *largest* of all 50 state. However this states population is very small. Only three other states ~~has~~ *have* fewer ~~person~~ *people* living in them Can you name this state," Is it alaska?" askd Al?

Unit 11 • Paragraph 44
Errors

Adjectives....... 1
Apostrophes 2
Capitalization 2
Commas........ 2
Periods......... 3
Plurals 2
Question
  Marks........ 1
Quotation
  Marks 2
Verbs 3

Total Errors: 18

~~~~~~

E B White writed such poppular childrens books as Charlotte's Web and stuart Little. White had sum trouble getting Stuart Little publishd. One book critic, in particular, thinked that it was awfull. Its a good thing that white didnt take that critics words to hart.

~~~~~~

I had never heared of a book called The Hunger Games until last Summer. Thats when my oldder sister read it. She said, Its fantastic You shood read it too." I like it so much that i readed all three book in the series. The othher two are called Catching Fire and Mockingjay.

E. B. White ~~writed~~ *wrote* such poppular childrens books as <u>Charlotte's Web</u> and <u>stuart Little</u>. White had ~~sum~~ *some* trouble getting <u>Stuart Little</u> publishd. One book critic, in particular, ~~thinked~~ *thought* that it was awfull. Its a good thing that white didnt take that critics words to hart.

Unit 12 • Paragraph 45
Errors

Apostrophes	 4
Capitalization	 2
Periods	 2
Spelling	 4
Underlines	 3
Verbs	 3

Total Errors: 18

I had never heared of a book called <u>The Hunger Games</u> until last Summer. Thats when my older sister read it. She said, "Its fantastic! You ~~shood~~ *should* read it too." I like it so much that i ~~readed~~ *read* all three book in the series. The other two are called <u>Catching Fire</u> and <u>Mockingjay</u>.

Unit 12 • Paragraph 46
Errors

Apostrophes	 2
Capitalization	 2
Commas	 1
Exclamation Points	 1
Plurals	 1
Quotation Marks	 1
Spelling	 3
Underlines	 3
Verbs	 3

Total Errors: 17

My cousins favorite moovie is The Lion King.

She watchs that film over and overr agin. She

especially love the music. Circle Of Life is the

song her likes mostest. Ive seened the movie

too. I thinks its just okay.

we seen a movie called Titanic. It was about

a enormous ship that sinked. The ship was also

named Titanic This shipp was the larggest at sea

when it beginned its voyage. No one thinked it

could be unnsafe. Then it hit a iceberg on April 15

1912. over 1,500 passengers and crew died

My cousins favorite moovie is <u>The Lion King.</u>
She watchs that film over and over agin. She
especially love the music. "Circle Of Life" is the
song her likes mostest. Ive seened the movie
too. I thinks its just okay.

Unit 12 • Paragraph 47 Errors

Adjectives	1
Apostrophes	3
Capitalization	1
Commas	1
Pronouns	1
Quotation Marks	2
Spelling	3
Underlines	1
Verbs	4

Total Errors: 17

we seen a movie called <u>Titanic.</u> It was about
a enormous ship that sinked. The ship was also
named <u>Titanic.</u> This ship was the larggest at sea
when it beginned its voyage. No one thinked it
could be unsafe. Then it hit a iceberg on April 15.
1912. over 1,500 passengers and crew died.

Unit 12 • Paragraph 48 Errors

Adjectives	1
Capitalization	2
Commas	1
Periods	2
Spelling	2
Underlines	2
Usage	2
Verbs	4

Total Errors: 16

Dad and me eight at a fancy restaurant last knight. The place settings were confuseing. For example I was gived three forks! Witch one should I use. Luckily, dad new that the fork on the outside is for eating sallad the one in the middle is fore dinner and the won on the inside is for desert.

The tiny cat scratchd at Mrs. Hunt's door. She bended down and looked at it's collar. "Whose pet is this," she wondered allowed. The tag told her that the cats name was Fluffy. Mrs Hunt smiled and said "I once have a cat with that name, to. I were much youngest back than!

Dad and ~~me eight~~ (I ate) at a fancy restaurant last ~~k~~night. The place settings were confus~~e~~ing. For example, I was give~~n~~ three forks! ~~Witch~~ (Which) one should I use? Luckily, ~~d~~ad ~~k~~new that the fork on the outside is for eating salad, the one in the middle is for~~e~~ dinner, and the ~~won~~ (one) on the inside is for desert~~s~~.

Unit 13 • Paragraph 49 Errors

Capitalization 1
Commas 3
Homophones 7
Pronouns 1
Question
  Marks 1
Spelling 1
Verbs 2

Total Errors: 16

The tiny cat scratch~~d~~ (scratche) at Mrs. Hunt's door. She ~~bended~~ (bent) down and looked at it's collar. "Whose pet is this?" she wondered ~~allowed~~ (aloud). The tag ~~telled~~ (told) her that the cat's name was Fluffy. Mrs. Hunt smiled and said, "I once ~~have~~ (had) a cat with that name, to~~o~~. I ~~were~~ (was) much ~~youngest~~ (younger) back than!"

Unit 13 • Paragraph 50 Errors

Adjectives 1
Apostrophes 1
Commas 1
Homophones 4
Periods 1
Question
  Marks 1
Quotation
  Marks 1
Verbs 5

Total Errors: 15

Ms. Ames teached us about the Red Sea today. Parts of the Red See are vary hot. Thats because their are volcanic vents on the seas floor. Heat come out of this vents. Ms Ames ended the lessen with a riddle. Her asked "when I drop a blue hat into the red Sea, what do it become." "Wet! I yelled out.

did you no that koala bears are not bear at all. They is more like kangaroos then bares. Fore example koalas have pouchs and live in australia. Also koala only eat the leafs from one type of tree. Can you imagine eatting just won thing all day. I wood eat ice cream

Ms. Ames ~~teached~~ *taught* us about the Red Sea today.

Parts of the Red Sea are *v*ary hot. Thats because

~~their~~ *there* are volcanic vents on the seas floor. Heat

come out of ~~this~~ *these* vents. Ms. Ames ended the lesson

with a riddle. ~~Her~~ *She* asked "when I drop a blue hat

into the red Sea, what ~~do~~ *does* it become." "Wet! I

yelled out.

Unit 13 • Paragraph 51 Errors

Apostrophes 2
Capitalization 2
Commas. 1
Homophones 4
Periods. 1
Pronouns 2
Question
  Marks. 1
Quotation
  Marks. 1
Verbs 3

Total Errors: 17

did you ~~no~~ *know* that koala bears are not bear at

all They ~~is~~ *are* more like kangaroos then ~~bares~~ *bears*. For

example koalas have pouchs and live in australia.

Also koala only eat the ~~leafs~~ *leaves* from one type of

tree. Can you imagine eatting just ~~won~~ *one* thing all

day I ~~wood~~ *would* eat ice cream

Unit 13 • Paragraph 52 Errors

Capitalization 2
Commas. 2
Homophones 6
Periods. 1
Plurals 4
Question
  Marks. 2
Verbs 2

Total Errors: 19

On July 20 1969 Neil Armstrong stepped out of a small spaceship. The spaceship was called Eagle. Mr Armstrong steped out of Eagle and he walk onto the moon he was the first person too ever do this. Neil planted a flag on the moon and he collected some moon rock wile he is there too.

Mr. Kim asked, Which state was the last to join the united states. In other words witch one is the 50th state?" Matt didnt know the answer but he new how to fined out. He used his computer to dew some research and there he discover that it were Hawaii. Matts familly had just goed there last Summer!

On July 20, 1969, Neil Armstrong stepped out of a small spaceship. The spaceship was called Eagle. Mr. Armstrong steped [P] out of Eagle and he walk [ed] onto the moon. he [=] was the first person too [,] ever do this. Neil planted a flag on the moon, and he collected some moon rock [s] wile [h] he is [was] there, too.

Unit 14 • Paragraph 53 Errors

Capitalization	 1
Commas	 5
Homophones	 2
Periods	 2
Plurals	 1
Spelling	 1
Underlines	 2
Verbs	 3

Total Errors: 17

Mr. Kim asked, ["] Which state was the last to join the united [=] states [=]? [?] In other words, witch [which] one is the 50th state?" Matt didn't [′] know the answer. but he new [k] how to fined [ɘ] out. He used his computer to dew [do] some research, and there he discover [ed] that it were [was] Hawaii. Matt's [′] familly [ɘ] had just goed [gone] there last Summer!

Unit 14 • Paragraph 54 Errors

Apostrophes	 2
Capitalization	 3
Commas	 3
Homophones	 4
Question Marks	 1
Quotation Marks	 1
Spelling	 1
Verbs	 3

Total Errors: 18

Unit 14
Paragraph
55

Deep in the jungle a group of ants marchs along. Suddenly, them come upon a large gap and they cannot jump across it. What do they dew. Sum of the ants links they legs together and they form a bridge the ants works as a teem too solve the problemm.

Unit 14
Paragraph
56

Deserts may bee the tougher places to live. They is hot and theres little water in them. However camel are maid for dessert liveing. Their coats reflect the light of the son and their humps storr fat. Even the unique shape of a camels blood cells allows there bloood to flow without much water

Deep in the jungle a group of ants marchs

along. Suddenly, there come upon a large gap

and they cannot jump across it. What do they

dew. Sum of the ants links they legs together

and they form a bridge the ants works as a

teem too solve the problemm.

Unit 14 • Paragraph 55
Errors

Capitalization 1
Commas 3
Homophones 4
Periods 1
Pronouns 2
Question
  Marks 1
Spelling 1
Verbs 3

Total Errors: 16

Deserts may bee the tougher places to live.

They is hot and theres little water in them.

However camel are maid for dessert liveing. Their

coats reflect the light of the son and their humps

story fat. Even the unique shape of a camels blood

cells allows there bloood to flow without much

water

Unit 14 • Paragraph 56
Errors

Adjectives 1
Apostrophes 2
Commas 3
Homophones 5
Periods 1
Plurals 1
Spelling 2
Verbs 2

Total Errors: 17

I couldn't never understand how someone could finish a triathlon. Inn my opinion there aren't no races that are toughest. The triathlon is the harder of them All. First, you swim in the see for 2.4 mile. Next you bisycle fore 112 miles. Lastly you running a entire marathon. Wow.

You wouldn't never guess that a egg could float in a glass of water, right. Well, heres a magic trick to try on you're friends. All you need is a egg a glass of water and a shaker of salt. Poor lots of salt into the glass of water and then drops the egg inn. The egg won't never sink the salt help it float.

I couldn't ~~never~~ understand how someone

could finish a triathlon. In~~n~~ my opinion, there

aren't ~~no~~ *any* races that are ~~toughest~~ *tougher*. The triathlon

is the ~~harder~~ *hardest* of them ~~A~~ll. First, you swim in

the sea *a* for 2.4 mile *s*. Next, you bisycle *c* for,

112 miles. Lastly, you ~~running~~ *run* a *n* entire

marathon. Wow !

Unit 15 • Paragraph 57 Errors

Adjectives	2
Capitalization	1
Commas	3
Double Negatives	2
Exclamation Points	1
Homophones	3
Plurals	1
Spelling	1
Usage	1
Verbs	1

Total Errors: 16

You ~~wouldn't~~ *would* never guess that a *n* egg could

float in a glass of water, right ? Well, heres *'* a

magic trick to try on ~~you're~~ *your* friends. All you need

is a *n* egg, a glass of water, and a shaker of salt.

Poor *u* lots of salt into the glass of water, and

then drops *'* the egg in *'*. The egg ~~won't~~ *will* never

sink, the salt help *s* it float.

Unit 15 • Paragraph 58 Errors

Apostrophes	1
Capitalization	1
Commas	3
Double Negatives	2
Homophones	3
Periods	1
Question Marks	1
Usage	2
Verbs	2

Total Errors: 16

When Ty was young his mother sitted him down. She say, I dont have very manny rules but you have to promiss you won't never do two thing." On that day, Ty sweared that he would'nt ever ride a motorcycle. The other thing she said he can't never do is bully someone. Ty agreeed to these rules and he hasn't done neither one yet.

Rex had livved in the city his hole life. He couldn't beleave he eyes when he spended a night at his cousins house in the country the sky was full of stars! Him hadn't saw nothing like it before. He ain't never been in a place wear there weren't no artificial lyghts.

When Ty was young his mother sitted [sat] him down. She say, [said] "I dont have very manhy rules but you have to promiss [promise] you won't [will] never do two things." On that day, Ty sweared [swore] that he would'nt ever ride a motorcycle. The other thing she said he can't never do is bully someone. Ty agreed to these rules and he hasn't done neither one yet.

Unit 15 • Paragraph 59
Errors

Apostrophes	2
Commas	3
Double Negatives	3
Plurals	1
Quotation Marks	1
Spelling	2
Verbs	4

Total Errors: 16

Rex had livved [lived] in the city his hole [whole] life. He couldn't beleave [believe] he [his] eyes when he spended [spent] a night at his cousins house in the country the sky was full of stars! Him [He] hadn't saw [seen] nothing [anything] like it before. He ain't [had] never been in a place wear [where] there weren't no [any] artificial lyghts [lights].

Unit 15 • Paragraph 60
Errors

Apostrophes	1
Capitalization	1
Double Negatives	3
Homophones	2
Periods	1
Pronouns	2
Spelling	2
Verbs	3

Total Errors: 15

My best friends grandma is the goodest cook I know. I have eated her food many time and it is always delishous. She makes a amazing pummkin soup every halloween and her make the tastyest turkey every thanksgiving. I never needs to be asked twice to eat dinner at grandma Alices house.

most people thinks insects is creepy and gross. Most couldn't never imajine eating one However, sum people use crickets mealworms termites and other insect as food. Them say that these insecks has a nutty flaver. Sounds tasty, doesnt it.

My best friends^' grandma is the ~~goodest~~ best cook I know. I have eated^n her food many time^s and it is always ~~delishous~~ delicious. She makes a^n amazing pum^pkin soup every halloween^, and ~~her~~ she make^s the tastyest^i turkey every thanksgiving. I never needs^' to be asked twice to eat dinner at grandma Alice^'s house.

Unit 16 • Paragraph 61 Errors

Adjectives	2
Apostrophes	2
Capitalization	3
Commas	2
Plurals	1
Pronouns	1
Spelling	2
Usage	1
Verbs	3

Total Errors: 17

most^= people thinks^' insects ~~is~~ are creepy and gross. Most ~~couldn't~~ could never imajine^g eating one^.However, ~~sum~~ some people use crickets^, mealworms^, termites^, and other insect^s as food. Ther^y say that these insec^ts has^have a nutty flaver^o. Sounds delicious, doesn^'t it^?

Unit 16 • Paragraph 62 Errors

Apostrophes	1
Capitalization	1
Commas	3
Double Negatives	1
Homophones	1
Periods	1
Plurals	1
Pronouns	1
Question Marks	1
Spelling	3
Verbs	3

Total Errors: 17

loch Ness is a lake in scotland. A legend say that a monster named Nessie was saw there long ago. Since then many has claimed to see nessie. A doctor named R K Wilson even taked a photo wilson's photo showed Nessies long neck comeing out of the water. The foto was later proven to bee a fake.

Thomas Edison was a famouss inventor. Hes best knowed for patenting a light bulb. edison once say, Genius is 1 percent inspiration and 99 persent perspiration. What do this mean It means that haveing a grate idea is important but a idea never becomes nothing without hard wurk

loch Ness is a lake in _scotland_. A legend say[s]

that a monster named Nessie was ~~saw~~ [seen] there long

ago. Since then[,] many ~~has~~ [have] claimed to see _nessie_.

A doctor named R[.] K[.] Wilson even ~~taked~~ [took] a photo[.]

wilson's photo showed Nessie['s] long neck com[e]ing

out of the water. The ~~foto~~ [photo] was later proven to

be[e] a fake.

Unit 16 • Paragraph 63
Errors

Apostrophes	1
Capitalization	4
Commas	1
Homophones	1
Periods	3
Spelling	1
Verbs	5

Total Errors: 16

Thomas Edison was a famous[s] inventor. He['s]

best ~~knowed~~ [known] for patenting a light bulb. _edison_

once ~~say~~ [said], [“]Genius is 1 percent inspiration and

99 per[c]ent perspiration.["] What do[es] this mean[?] It

means that hav[e]ing a ~~grate~~ [great] idea is important[,]

but a[n] idea never becomes ~~nothing~~ [anything] without

hard w[o]rk[.]

Unit 16 • Paragraph 64
Errors

Apostrophes	1
Capitalization	1
Commas	1
Double Negatives	1
Homophones	1
Question Marks	1
Quotation Marks	2
Periods	1
Spelling	3
Usage	1
Verbs	4

Total Errors: 17

Some whales swims up to Alaska durring the summer. There is lots of fishes to eat their but the whales must be carefull to leave the area before Winter. Whales are giant mammals and mammal need air to breethe. The water near alaska may freeze over and the wales will be trap under the ice

Beavers are sum of the goodest builders in the animal kingdom. To build there homes, they began by draging logs into stream. this block the floww of water and makes ponds. Next beavers use they sharp tooths to cut down small tree. Beavers homes are made of wood and mudd.

Some whales swims up to Alaska durring the summer. There is lots of fishes to eat their but the whales must be carefull to leave the area before Winter. Whales are giant mammals and mammal need air to breethe. The water near alaska may freeze over and the wales will be trap under the ice.

Unit 17 • Paragraph 65 Errors

Capitalization 2
Commas 3
Homophones 1
Periods 1
Plurals 2
Spelling 4
Verbs 3

Total Errors: 16

Beavers are sum of the goodest builders in the animal kingdom. To build there homes, they began by draging logs into stream. this block the flowy of water and makes ponds. Next beavers use they sharp tooths to cut down small tree. Beavers homes are made of wood and mudd.

Unit 17 • Paragraph 66 Errors

Adjectives 1
Apostrophes 1
Capitalization 1
Commas 1
Homophones 2
Plurals 3
Pronouns 1
Spelling 2
Verbs 3

Total Errors: 15

I readed somewhere that a spiders silk is strongest than steal. That seams incredible. Also some spiders can spin up to ate different kind of silk. Some silk is very sticky and this is the silk that is used for catching food small insects become pray when them get cot in webs maid from this stickey silk.

Ken like to test his friends to see what them no. He asked "Which animal can live the longest." I had just learned this bit of trivia, so I says, no animal lives longest than the tortoise. It can survvive four over 200 year." Ken gaspped, "Your right! I thinked me was the only one who new that.

I ~~readed~~ *read* somewhere that a spiders' silk is ~~strongest~~ *stronger* than steal. That seams incredible. Also, some spiders can spin up to ~~ate~~ *eight* different kinds of silk. Some silk is very sticky, and this is the silk that is used for catching food. small insects become pray when them get ~~cot~~ *caught* in webs ~~maid~~ *made* from this stickey silk.

Unit 17 • Paragraph 67
Errors

Adjectives 1
Apostrophes 1
Capitalization 1
Commas 2
Homophones 6
Periods 1
Plurals 1
Pronouns 1
Spelling 2
Verbs 1

Total Errors: 17

Ken ~~like~~ *likes* to test his friends to see what ~~them~~ *they* ~~no~~ *know*. He asked, "Which animal can live the longest?" I had just learned this bit of trivia, so I ~~says~~ *said*, "no animal lives ~~longest~~ *longer* than the tortoise. It can ~~survvive~~ *survive* ~~four~~ *over* 200 years." Ken gaspped, "~~Your~~ *You're* right! I ~~thinked~~ *thought* ~~me~~ *I* was the only one who ~~new~~ *knew* that."

Unit 17 • Paragraph 68
Errors

Adjectives 1
Capitalization 1
Commas 1
Homophones 4
Plurals 1
Pronouns 2
Question
  Marks 1
Quotation
  Marks 2
Spelling 1
Verbs 4

Total Errors: 18

My brother love his car. Yo'ull never sea someone take gooder care of a vehical than he do. He washs and waxs it every saturday. He tests the headlights checks the oil, and puts err in the tires once a weak too. It's fare to say that he spend more time cleaning the car then he does driveing it.

Ann And Eve goed shopping at Greenwood mall. Eve said, Wow, these sail prices are amazing. Are you going too buy anything Ann? Ann thinked for a momment and said "There isn't nothing I need write now. Besides, Im saveing my money to by a nice winter coat

My brother love[s] his car. Yo[u']ll never sea[e]
someone take ~~gooder~~ [better] care of a ~~vehical~~ [vehicle] than he
do[es]. He wash[e]s and wax[e]s it every saturday. He
tests the headlights[,] checks the oil, and puts ~~err~~ [air]
in the tires once a weak[e] too. It's ~~fare~~ [fair] to say
that he spend[s] more time cleaning the car then[a]
he does driv[e]ing it.

Unit 18 • Paragraph 69 Errors

Adjectives. 1
Apostrophes 1
Capitalization 1
Commas. 2
Homophones 5
Spelling 1
Verbs 6

Total Errors: 17

Ann [A]nd Eve ~~goed~~ [went] shopping at Greenwood mall.
Eve said, ["]Wow, these ~~sail~~ [sale] prices are amazing[!] Are
you going to[o] buy anything[,] Ann[?"] Ann ~~thinked~~ [thought] for
a mom[e]ent and said[,] "There isn't ~~nothing~~ [anything] I need
~~write~~ [right] now. Besides, I[']m sav[e]ing my money to by[u]
a nice winter coat[."]

Unit 18 • Paragraph 70 Errors

Apostrophes 1
Capitalization 2
Commas. 2
Double
  Negatives. 1
Exclamation
  Points. 1
Homophones 4
Periods. 1
Quotation
  Marks. 3
Spelling 1
Verbs 3

Total Errors: 19

Jim herd a skratch at his door late one knight.

Whose there," he whispered. No one answer, so

he said it loudest this time. "Who is it." Sudenly,

they're was a thud on the door. Jim could'nt

weight any longer. He swinged the door open

his dog looked up at him and waged its tale.

Leah Pedro and I spend severel SAturdays

each summer cleaning up local beachs. The three

of we belongs to a group who's goal is to keep

are shores clean the work mite be hard but

wee barely notice that. There isn't no place

weed rather be on a warm Summer day

Paragraph 71

Jim herd a skratch at his door late one knight.
(*a* above herd, *c* above skratch, *g* above knight)

"Whose there," he whispered. No one answer, so
(*" Who's* above Whose, *?* and *g* marks, *ed* above answer)

he said it loudest this time. "Who is it." Sudenly,
(*louder* above loudest, *?* and *d* marks)

they're was a thud on the door. Jim could'nt
(*there* above they're, *g* and *l* marks)

weight any longer. He swinged the door open
(*wait* above weight, *swung* above swinged, period mark)

his dog looked up at him and waged its tale.
(*g* above waged, *tail* above tale)

Unit 18 • Paragraph 71 Errors	
Adjectives	1
Apostrophes	1
Capitalization	1
Homophones	6
Periods	1
Question Marks	2
Quotation Marks	1
Spelling	2
Verbs	3

Total Errors: 18

Paragraph 72

Leah Pedro and I spend severel Saturdays
(*a* above Saturdays, comma marks)

each summer cleaning up local beachs. The three
(*e* above beachs)

of we belongs to a group who's goal is to keep
(*us* above we, *whose* above who's)

are shores clean the work mite be hard but
(*our* above are, *might* above mite, period/comma marks)

wee barely notice that. There isn't no place
(*is* above isn't)

weed rather be on a warm Summer day
(*we'd* above weed, period mark)

Unit 18 • Paragraph 72 Errors	
Capitalization	3
Commas	3
Double Negatives	1
Homophones	5
Periods	2
Plurals	1
Pronouns	1
Spelling	1
Verbs	1

Total Errors: 18

Cowboy hats may be fashion statement but the'yre also kwite usefull. For starters a cowboy hat has a wide brim this protects the cowboys eyes, face, and necks from sun snow and rein. Cowboy hats has hi crowns too. This helps cowboy's carry food or water in there upside-down hats.

Subways is railroads that run under citys. The first subway was builded in London England in 1863. Weave come a long weigh since then. Now theres even a subway that runs under water fore over 20 mile it is called the Channel Tunnel and it connect the countrys of france and england

Cowboy hats may be fashion statement**s** but

the**'**yre also ~~kwite~~ *quite* usefull**.** For starters**,** a cowboy

hat has a wide brim**.** this protects the cowboy**'s**

eyes, face, and neck**s** from sun**,** snow**,** and ~~rein~~ *rain.*

Cowboy hats ~~has~~ *have* hi**gh** crowns**,** too. This helps

cowboy**'s** carry food or water in ~~there~~ *their*

upside-down hats.

Unit 19 • Paragraph 73
Errors

Apostrophes	3
Capitalization	1
Commas	5
Homophones	3
Periods	1
Plurals	2
Spelling	2
Verbs	1

Total Errors: 18

Subways ~~is~~ *are* railroads that run under ~~citys~~ *cities*. The

first subway was ~~builded~~ *built* in London**,** England**,** in

1863. ~~Weave~~ *We've* come a long ~~weigh~~ *way* since then. Now

there**'s** even a subway that runs under water for**e**

over 20 mile**s.** it is called the Channel Tunnel**,** and

it connect**s** the ~~countrys~~ *countries* of **f**rance and **e**ngland**.**

Unit 19 • Paragraph 74
Errors

Apostrophes	1
Capitalization	3
Commas	3
Homophones	3
Periods	2
Plurals	3
Verbs	3

Total Errors: 18

Id never rided a horse unttil today. I was a

guessed at a ranch near Pueblo Colorado. All of

the other guests road horses with name like

Lightning and wilder. I was gived a horse named

Turtle. I guess the cowboys could sea that I

were afrayed of going to fast! Tertle was the

perffect horse for Me

Mom has been takeing pottery clases on

Thursdays for a wile now. Shes getting best each

weak at makeing cups bowls and dishs from clay.

Moms latest creation was a urn that she paint

orange and blew. An earn looks just like a vase

to me but I do'nt no much about these thing.

Id never ~~rided~~ *ridden* a horse unttil today. I was a

~~guessed~~ *guest* at a ranch near Pueblo Colorado. All of

the other guests ~~road~~ *rode* horses with name *s* like

Lightning and wilder. I was gived *n* a horse named

Turtle. I guess the cowboys could see *e* that I

~~were~~ *was* ~~afrayed~~ *afraid* of going to *o* fast! Tertle *u* was the

perffect horse for Me.

Unit 19 • Paragraph 75
Errors

Apostrophes 1
Capitalization 2
Commas. 1
Homophones 4
Periods. 1
Plurals 1
Spelling 4
Verbs 3

Total Errors: 17

Mom has been takeing pottery clases *s* on

Thursdays for a wile *h* now. Shes *j* getting ~~best~~ *better* each

weak *e* at makeing cups bowls and dishs *e* from clay.

Moms latest creation was a *n* urn that she paint *ed*

orange and ~~blew.~~ *blue.* An ~~earn~~ *urn* looks just like a vase

to me but I do'nt *j* ~~no~~ *know* much about these thing. *s*

Unit 19 • Paragraph 76
Errors

Adjectives. 1
Apostrophes 3
Commas. 3
Homophones 5
Plurals 3
Usage 1
Verbs 3

Total Errors: 19

Has you heared of Kitty Hawk, North carolina. Something famous happenned there on december 17 1903. Kitty hawk is the town wear the two Wright brothers flied the first engine-powered airplane the first flite of the wright brother's plain stayed in the air for just twelve second.

Kay and Lisa beginned selling lemonade at 930 a m. It already was a hot day and the too friends hoped to cell a lot of drink. Something was'nt rite, though. The first customer took a sip spit it out, and through away his cup. Kay tryed the lemonaid. She frowned and said, Lisa I think us use salt instedd of sugar!

Have
~~Has~~ you heard of Kitty Hawk, North carolina?

Something famous happenned there on december

17, 1903. Kitty hawk is the town where ~~wear~~ the two

flew
Wright brothers ~~flied~~ the first engine-powered

flight
airplane. the first ~~flite~~ of the wright brother's

plane
~~plain~~ stayed in the air for just twelve seconds.

Unit 20 • Paragraph 77
Errors

Apostrophes	1
Capitalization	5
Commas	1
Homophones	2
Periods	1
Plurals	1
Question Marks	1
Spelling	1
Verbs	4

Total Errors: 17

---

began
Kay and Lisa ~~beginned~~ selling lemonade at

9:30 a. m. It already was a hot day, and the two ~~too~~

sell
friends hoped to ~~cell~~ a lot of drinks. Something

right
was'nt ~~rite~~, though. The first customer took a sip,

threw
spit it out, and ~~through~~ away his cup. Kay tried ~~tryed~~

lemonade "
the ~~lemonaid~~. She frowned and said, Lisa, I think

we d a "
~~us~~ use salt instedd of sugar!"

Unit 20 • Paragraph 78
Errors

Apostrophes	1
Colons	1
Commas	3
Homophones	4
Periods	1
Plurals	1
Pronouns	1
Quotation Marks	2
Spelling	2
Verbs	3

Total Errors: 19

Dad was searching thru all of his pocket as he said, Has anyone see my keys. Mom Chris and I shaked our head. "They must be around hear somewhere" said Chris We begin looking in every place we could think off. Finally Mom find Dads' keyes. They was sticking out of the front door.

Emma was fulled with excitement. Tonite, her was going to Radio City Music Hall to sea a musical. Radio city music hall is the bigger theater on earth. There is no biggest curtain than it's stage curtan. Emma new that tonights show would bee a treat and she could'nt weight to go

Dad was searching ~~thru~~ through all of his pocket**s** as

he said, " Has anyone see**n** my keys?" Mom, Chris, and

I ~~shaked~~ shook our head**s**. "They must be around ~~hear~~ here

somewhere," said Chris. We begin looking in every

place we could think off. Finally, Mom ~~find~~ found Dads'

keyes. They ~~was~~ were sticking out of the front door.

**Unit 20 • Paragraph 79
Errors**

Apostrophes	1
Commas	4
Homophones	1
Periods	1
Plurals	3
Question Marks	1
Quotation Marks	2
Spelling	2
Verbs	5

Total Errors: 20

Emma was fulled with excitement. ~~Tonite, her~~ Tonight she

was going to Radio City Music Hall to se**e** a

musical. Radio city music hall is the ~~bigger~~ biggest theater

on earth. There is no ~~biggest~~ bigger curtain than it's

stage curtan. Emma new that tonights show would

bee a treat, and she could'nt ~~weight~~ wait to go.

**Unit 20 • Paragraph 80
Errors**

Adjectives	2
Apostrophes	2
Capitalization	4
Commas	1
Homophones	5
Periods	1
Pronouns	1
Spelling	2
Verbs	1

Total Errors: 19

Yesterday Patty and me packd a picnic lunch and taked it to pine park everything started out grate. The food was delicious the whether was warm and we was smiling. Thats when a army of aunts invaded our area. Thems tiny critters marchd across our blanket and, right onto are plates!

When grandpa jack was a youngest man, he offen fishd off of Sunrise Pier. Youd sea crowds of fishermans along that peer in those day. Grandpa Jack would arrive by 530 a m and not leave untill almost dark. Than he would gather his pole and his bucket of fish and he'd head home four dinner?

Yesterday Patty and me packd a picnic lunch [I] [e]

and taked it to pine park everything started out [took]

grate. The food was delicious the whether was [great] [weather]

warm and we was smiling. Thats when a army [were] [n]

of aunts invaded our area. Thems tiny critters [Those]

marchd across our blanket and right onto [e]

are plates! [our]

Unit 21 • Paragraph 81 Errors

Apostrophes	 1
Capitalization	 3
Commas	 4
Homophones	 4
Periods	 1
Pronouns	 2
Usage	 1
Verbs	 4

Total Errors: 20

When grandpa jack was a youngest man, he [younger]

offen fishd off of Sunrise Pier. Youd sea crowds [t] [e] [e]

of fishermans along that peer in those day. [fishermen] [i] [s]

Grandpa Jack would arrive by 530 a m and not [:]

leave untill almost dark. Than he would gather [e]

his pole and his bucket of fish and he'd head

home four dinner?

Unit 21 • Paragraph 82 Errors

Adjectives	 1
Apostrophes	 1
Capitalization	 2
Colons	 1
Commas	 1
Homophones	 4
Periods	 3
Plurals	 2
Spelling	 2
Verbs	 1

Total Errors: 18

Shanes studying the bones of the human boddy

for tomorrows quiz. He usually do well on theese

quizes but he's worryed about this won. "I dont

know the name of all the bones" fretted Shane.

Tom said "Adults has 206 bone. Will you bee

expected to know all of them?

Tom asked "How could one be warm in a

house maid of snow." Mr. Clark was teaching

Toms class about igloos. Mr. Clark said "good

question tom. Think of a igloo like it's a blanket

a blanket doesnt make heat but it do keep the

heet from ur body close to you. It allso keep

cold err away from you.

Shanes studying the bones of the human boddy

for tomorrows quiz. He usually do well on theese

quizes but he's worryed about this won. "I dont

know the name of all the bones" fretted Shane.

Tom said "Adults has 206 bone. Will you bee

expected to know all of them?"

Unit 21 • Paragraph 83 Errors

Apostrophes	3
Commas	3
Homophones	2
Plurals	3
Quotation Marks	1
Spelling	2
Verbs	3

Total Errors: 17

Tom asked "How could one be warm in a

house maid of snow," Mr. Clark was teaching

Toms class about igloos. Mr. Clark said "good

question tom. Think of a igloo like it's a blanket

a blanket doesnt make heat but it do keep the

heet from ur body close to you. It allso keep

cold err away from you."

Unit 21 • Paragraph 84 Errors

Apostrophes	2
Capitalization	3
Commas	4
Homophones	2
Periods	1
Question Marks	1
Quotation Marks	1
Spelling	3
Usage	1
Verbs	2

Total Errors: 20

Dad and I was hikeing near Mt Shasta when we seen a deer and her childs. Dad put his finger to him lips and i knew that meaned that we should be quite. I try my harderest to not make no sounds but just then my shoo crunchd down on some leafs. The dear and her babys runned off into the woods.

Me aunt and Uncle should be prowed of themselfs. They just open a bakery on Ninth st, which is rite near there house the hole family is sew excited for them! Weve always beleeved that my ant's cookies cakes and breads was the goodest in town.

Dad and I ~~was~~ **were** hikeing near Mt. Shasta when

we ~~seen~~ **saw** a deer and her ~~childs.~~ **children** Dad put his finger

to him **s** lips and ~~i~~ **i** knew that ~~meaned~~ **meant** that we

should be ~~quite.~~ **quiet** I ~~try~~ **tried** my ~~harderest~~ **hardest** to not make

~~no~~ **any** sounds but just then my shoe **e** crunchd **e** down

on some ~~leafs.~~ **leaves** The ~~dear~~ **e** and her ~~babys~~ **babies** ~~runned~~ **ran**

off into the woods.

~~Me~~ **y** aunt and ~~u~~ ncle should be ~~prowed~~ **proud** of

~~themselfs.~~ **themselves** They just open **ed** a bakery on Ninth ~~st,~~ **st,**

which is ~~rite~~ **right** near ~~there~~ **their** house the **w** ~~hole~~ **whole** family

is ~~sow~~ **so** excited for them! We've always beleeved **i**

that my ~~ant's~~ **u** cookies cakes and breads ~~was~~ **are**

the ~~goodest~~ **best** in town.

~~~~~~

On Thursday, Jannuary 9 we will face the Pittsville Panthers in a importent footballl game. Each teem is vary confident that it will bee the winner. We believe in ourselfs and i know that the panthers believe in theyselves, to. Who will win. I cant weight to fined out?

~~~~~~

Matt lookd at heself in the miror and said I need a haircut" He did some research to find the cheaperest barbershop near his hous. The most close shop got many aweful review, tho. He decide to give it a try anyway. Boy was matt sorry he done that! His knew haircut did knot look good.

On Thursday, January 9 we will face the

Pittsville Panthers in a important football game.

Each teem is vary confident that it will bee the

winner. We believe in ~~ourselfs~~ *ourselves* and i know that

the panthers believe in theyselves, to. Who will

win. I cant ~~weight~~ *wait* to fined out?

Unit 22 • Paragraph 87 Errors

Apostrophes	1
Capitalization	2
Commas	2
Exclamation Points	1
Homophones	6
Pronouns	2
Question Marks	1
Spelling	3
Usage	1

Total Errors: 19

Matt lookd at ~~heself~~ *himself* in the miror and said

"I need a haircut" He did some research to find

the ~~cheaperest~~ *cheapest* barbershop near his hous. The

~~most close~~ *closest* shop got many aweful review, ~~tho.~~ *though*

He decide to give it a try anyway. Boy was

matt sorry he ~~done~~ *did* that! His knew haircut

did knot look good.

Unit 22 • Paragraph 88 Errors

Adjectives	2
Capitalization	1
Commas	2
Homophones	2
Periods	1
Plurals	1
Pronouns	1
Quotation Marks	1
Spelling	4
Verbs	3

Total Errors: 18

Sam studys snakes, so he nose a lot about them. However I was shure he was mixxing up his facts when he sweared that a snake can growed to be over thirty foots long. Thats moore than three time longer then the worlds taller man! Then I checkd sams claims and they was tru.

Germs can make you sic germs gets into the air from sneezeing coughing, and breathin. Them also gets on surfaces like doornobs, bed sheet, and Cell fones. Thats why scrubing your hands with warm water and sope is necessery. You should also cover ur nos and mouthe whenever you sneeze or coff.

Sam ~~studys~~ *studies* snakes, so he ~~nose~~ *knows* a lot about them. However, I was ~~shure~~ *sure* he was ~~mixxing~~ *mixing* up his facts when he ~~sweared~~ *swore* that a snake can ~~growed~~ *grow* to be over thirty ~~foots~~ *feet* long. That's ~~moore~~ *more* than three time*s* longer the*a*n the world's ~~taller~~ *tallest* man! Then I check*e*d sam*'s* claims, and they ~~was~~ *were* tru*e*.

Unit 23 • Paragraph 89 Errors

Adjectives	1
Apostrophes	3
Capitalization	1
Commas	2
Homophones	2
Plurals	2
Spelling	3
Verbs	6

Total Errors: 20

Germs can make you sic*k*, germs gets into the air from ~~sneezeing~~ *sneezing*, coughing, and breathin*g*. Them also gets on surfaces like doornobs, bed sheet*s*, and *C*ell ~~fones~~ *phones*. That's why scrubbing your hands with warm water and ~~sope~~ *soap* is necess*a*ry. You should also cover ~~ur~~ *your* nos*e* and mouth*e* whenever you sneeze or ~~coff~~ *cough*.

Unit 23 • Paragraph 90 Errors

Apostrophes	1
Capitalization	2
Commas	1
Homophones	1
Periods	1
Plurals	1
Pronouns	1
Spelling	8
Verbs	5

Total Errors: 21

Beeing a astronaut sounds very excsiting and it is. Astronauts though, mussed deal with difficultys as they dew they jobs. For example its hardder to sleep in space. As astronots circle earth, they may sea five or sicks sunrise every eight ours!

a famous photographer is visitting are school next weak his fotos have bean showed in art gallerys and museums. They has also appeared in such maggazines as Life, Time, and Newsweek. I hope he tell us many storys about heself and how he growed up to be such a amazing arttist

Beeing a astronaut sounds very excsiting

and it is. Astronauts, though, mussed deal with
(must)

difficultys as they dew they jobs. For example, its
(difficulties) *(do)* *(their)*

hardder to sleep in space. As astronots circle
(astronauts)

earth, they may sea five or sicks sunrise every

eight ours!

Unit 23 • Paragraph 91
Errors

Apostrophes	1
Capitalization	1
Commas	3
Homophones	5
Plurals	2
Pronouns	1
Spelling	3
Usage	1
Verbs	1

Total Errors: 18

---

a famous photographer is visitting are school
(our)

next weak his fotos have bean showed in art
(photos) *(shown)*

gallerys and museums. They has also appeared in
(galleries) *(have)*

such maggazines as <u>Life</u>, <u>Time</u>, and <u>Newsweek</u>. I

hope he tell us many storys about heself and how
(stories) *(himself)*

he growed up to be such a amazing arttist.
(grew)

Unit 23 • Paragraph 92
Errors

Capitalization	2
Homophones	3
Periods	2
Plurals	2
Pronouns	1
Spelling	3
Underlines	3
Usage	1
Verbs	5

Total Errors: 22

two famous german composers is Beethoven and Bach. They are both classical composer who lived in the eighteenth sentury amazingly beethoven creatted severel masterpiece after him had losed his hearring. Don't that sound compleately immpossible.

Theres a famuss ocean liner anchored in Long beach california. It is called Queen Mary, and some say it's haunted and fillled with goasts. Back in its day however Queen Mary was a ocean liner that saled all around the atlantic ocean. It's first voyyage taked place on may 27 1936

two famous german composers ~~is~~ (are) Beethoven

and Bach. They are both classical composer(s) who

lived in the eighteenth (c)entury. amazingly, (b)eethoven

creatted sever(a)l masterpiece(s) after ~~him~~ (he) had ~~losed~~ (lost)

his hearring. ~~Don't~~ (Doesn't) that sound compleately

immpossible. (?)

**Unit 24 • Paragraph 93
Errors**

Capitalization 4
Commas........ 1
Periods......... 1
Plurals 2
Pronouns 1
Question
  Marks......... 1
Spelling 5
Verbs 4

Total Errors: 19

There's a ~~famuss~~ (famous) ocean liner anchored in Long

beach(,) california. It is called <u>Queen Mary</u>, and

some say it's haunted and fillied with ~~goasts.~~ (ghosts)

Back in its day(,) however(,) <u>Queen Mary</u> was a(n)

ocean liner that sal(i)ed all around the atlantic

ocean. It's first voyyage ~~taked~~ (took) place on

may 27(,) 1936(.)

**Unit 24 • Paragraph 94
Errors**

Apostrophes 1
Capitalization 5
Commas........ 4
Homophones 1
Periods......... 1
Spelling 4
Underlines 2
Usage 1
Verbs 2

Total Errors: 21

Geting reggular exercise is vary important.
Activitys like running jogging and hiking keeps
your hart healthy. Lifting waits helps u build
strong mussels. To loose weight you has to
burn more calorie thru exersize than you take
in threw Food

My sister was so sic last nite. She have a
runny nose a soar throat and a fever of an
hundred and two degree. Mom called dr Stanley
and he gived us some addvice on how too nurse
my sisster back to helth. Luckily she waked up
feeling bester this mourning.

Geting reggular exercise is vary important.
(t, g corrections; e above vary)

Activitys **like running jogging and hiking keeps**
(Activities; commas after running, jogging; s correction on keeps)

your hart healthy. Lifting waits **helps** u **build**
(t above hart; weights above waits; you above u)

strong mussels. **To** loose **weight you** has **to**
(muscles above mussels; s correction; comma after weight; have above has)

burn more calorie thru exersize **than you take**
(s through exercise above thru exersize)

in threw **Food.**
(through above threw; period)

Unit 24 • Paragraph 95 Errors

Capitalization	1
Commas.	3
Homophones	6
Periods.	1
Plurals	2
Spelling	4
Verbs	3

Total Errors: 20

My sister was so sic **last** nite. **She** have **a**
(k above sic; night above nite; had above have)

runny nose a soar **throat and a fever of a**n
(sore above soar; commas; n correction)

hundred and two degree. Mom called dr **Stanley**
(s above degree; Dr. correction; period after Stanley)

and he gived **us some** addvice **on how** too **nurse**
(gave above gived; advice; to above too)

my sisster **back to** helth. **Luckily she** waked **up**
(sister; health; comma after Luckily; woke above waked)

feeling bester **this** mourning.
(better; morning above mourning)

Unit 24 • Paragraph 96 Errors

Adjectives.	1
Capitalization	1
Commas.	4
Homophones	4
Periods.	1
Plurals	1
Spelling	4
Usage	1
Verbs	3

Total Errors: 20

Mr. Shaw walked up to the bored, pickt up a peace of chalk, and rote a question their. He wrote "How manny months names begin with a vowl letter." Josh razed his hand and say, "The answer is Three. Them are april august and october." "Good job Josh!" said Mr Shaw.

Dad and me couldnt belief it. We pinchd ourselfs to see if we was dreaming. No wee were wide awake. I rubed my eyes and taked a closest look. The purpel dress I had dreemed of waring was in the stores window. Best of all it was on sail! Dad smile and said, Lets by it now!

                                  board   picked
Mr. Shaw walked up to the ~~bored~~, ~~pickt~~ up

       piece   there
a ~~peace~~ of chalk, and rote a question ~~their~~. He

wrote "How manny months names begin with

          e   raised   said
a vowl letter," Josh ~~razed~~ his hand and ~~say~~,

"The answer is Three. Them are april august

and october." "Good job Josh!" said Mr Shaw.

Unit 25 • Paragraph 97 Errors

Apostrophes	1
Capitalization	4
Commas	4
Homophones	5
Periods	1
Pronouns	1
Question Marks	1
Spelling	2
Verbs	2

Total Errors: 21

                  I   believe
Dad and ~~me~~ couldnt ~~belief~~ it. We pinchd

ourselves   were
~~ourselfs~~ to see if we ~~was~~ dreaming. No wee were

                                   b   took   closer
wide awake. I rubed my eyes and ~~taked~~ a ~~closest~~

         purple   a   e
look. The ~~purpel~~ dress I had dreemed of waring

was in the stores window. Best of all it was on

sale   d
~~sail~~! Dad smile and said, "Lets by it now!"

Unit 25 • Paragraph 98 Errors

Adjectives	1
Apostrophes	3
Commas	2
Homophones	3
Pronouns	2
Quotation Marks	2
Spelling	3
Verbs	6

Total Errors: 22

I knowed somethin was wierd when both of my friend excused theyselves from the tabel at bert's Barbeque Cafe. When they returnd a bunch of waitors were following behined them. Then everyone singed Happy birthday to You really loudly I blushd and hided my face in me hands

Wow did you know that kids have they own holiday, in Japan. Its called Children's Day and it's on may 5 everry year. That day is set aside to celabrate childs and they're happyness. Childrens day has bin a national holliday since the japanese goverment make it one in 1948

knew
I ~~knowed~~ somethin$_g$ was ~~wierd~~ weird when both of

s   m   table
my friend excused theyselves from the ~~tabel~~ at

e
bert's Barbeque Cafe. When they returnd a bunch

e   hid
of waitors were following behined them. Then

sang
everyone ~~singed~~ "Happy birthday to You" really

e   hid
loudly I blushd and ~~bided~~ my face in me hands.

Unit 25 • Paragraph 99
Errors

Capitalization 2
Commas 1
Periods 2
Plurals 1
Pronouns 2
Quotation
 Marks 2
Spelling 5
Verbs 5

Total Errors: 20

---

their
Wow, did you know that kids have ~~they~~ own

holiday, in Japan. Its called Children's Day and it's

everry
on may 5 everry year. That day is set aside to

e   children   their
celabrate ~~childs~~ and ~~they're~~ happyness. Childrens

been
day has ~~bin~~ a national holliday since the japanese

n   d
goverment make it one in 1948.

Unit 25 • Paragraph 100
Errors

Apostrophes 2
Capitalization 3
Commas 3
Homophones 2
Periods 1
Plurals 1
Pronouns 1
Question
 Marks 1
Spelling 5
Verbs 1

Total Errors: 20

Editing Marks

Here is a list of the editing marks that are used in this book.

Mark	Meaning	Example
≡	Capitalize	We visited france.
/	Lowercase	It is Summer.
∧	Insert	We at tacos today.
℘	Delete	I likes that movie.
⊙	Add Period	I am here⊙
?	Add Question Mark	Who is it?
!	Add Exclamation Point	Watch out!
①	Add Comma	He lives in Ames Iowa.
:	Add Colon	I woke up at 630.
'	Add Apostrophe	That is Bobs hat.
" "	Add Quotation Mark	I said, "See you soon."
———	Add Underline	I saw Star Wars twice.